# Science Experiments

 WITH

# MAGNETS

## Sally Nankivell-Aston
## and Dorothy Jackson

W
# FRANKLIN WATTS
### A Division of Grolier Publishing
NEW YORK • LONDON • HONG KONG • SYDNEY
DANBURY, CONNECTICUT

Picture credits: Science Photo Library 10 (bl Geoff Lane/CSIRO); Still Pictures 13 (tm Andre Maslennikov); Science Photo Library 23 (mr Geoff Tompkinson); Telegraph Colour Library 25 (tr), 29 (br); The Stock Market 27 (tr).

Thanks, too, to our models: Kreena Davy, Aaron Gupta, Jordan Leatherland, George Marney, Charlotte Sipi and Beau-Bart Von Haidenthaler.

Editor: Claire Berridge
Art director: Jonathan Hair
Designer: Richard Langford
Picture research: Sue Mennell
Photography: Ray Moller
(unless otherwise credited)
Cover photography: Steve Shott
Artwork: Sean Wilkinson

First published in 1999 by Franklin Watts

First American edition 2000 by Franklin Watts/Children's Press
A Division of Grolier Publishing
90 Sherman Turnpike
Danbury
CT 06816

ISBN 0-531-14576-X (hbk)
        0-531-15430-0 (pbk)

Catalogue information available from the Library of Congress

Visit Franklin Watts/Children's Press on the Internet at:
http://publishing.grolier.com

2

# Contents

# Magnets Everywhere

A MAGNET IS A MATERIAL THAT ATTRACTS certain metals. The invisible force of attraction is called magnetism. It is named after the magnetic rock called lodestone or magnetite. This rock has been known about for over two thousand years. Magnets have fascinated people ever since they were found. In this book you can find out much more about magnets and what they can do.

You may be surprised to know that all the things you see on this page use a magnet. Magnets are very important to us in our everyday lives. Look around you and spot how many things have magnets in them. How many did you see?

## Be Amazed

Amaze yourself and your friends with experiments using magnets. You will find out more about the invisible force of magnetism and what magnets are used for. Some experiments may help answer questions you already ask about magnets. Some may make you think of more!

## Look Closely

Scientists always ask lots of questions and observe carefully. When you are doing the experiments, look closely to see what is happening. Don't be upset if your predictions do not always turn out as you had thought. Scientists (and that includes you!) learn a lot from unexpected results.

## Be Careful

Always let an adult know that you are doing an experiment. Ask for help if you need to cut something, use batteries, or handle heavy or sharp objects. Keep your magnet away from machines and equipment (such as the television) — magnetism can damage them. Follow the step-by-step instructions carefully.

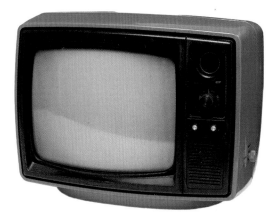

# Fun with Magnets

W**ITH THESE FIRST SIMPLE** experiments you can begin to find out about some of the things that magnets can do and see how the invisible force of magnetism makes the magnets move around.

✔ You will need
- ✔ two magnets (same size and type)
- ✔ a tabletop or other flat surface
- ✔ ruler

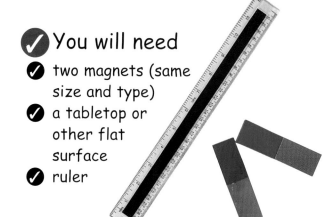

## In Action

The push and pull of magnets is used to make some toys work. For example, in some train sets, the engines, carriages, and trucks have magnets on each end. Children playing with the train can use the magnets to stick the train parts together or to push them away.

**1** Put the two magnets on the table. Can you use one magnet to pull the other toward it and make them "stick" together? Can you make one push the other away, without them even touching? What did you do to make these things happen?

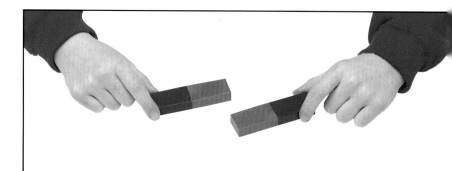

**2** Repeat what you did in step 1 but this time hold the magnets as they pull together and then as they push apart. Can you feel the magnetic force pushing and pulling? Does it feel strong or weak?

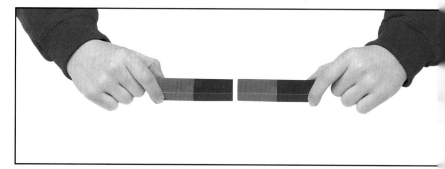

**3** Now place one of the magnets on the table. Hold the other high above and gently lower it toward the magnet on the table until it makes the lower magnet jump. Use the ruler to measure how high the magnet jumps.

**4** Look closely to see what happens when the magnet jumps. Did it flip over? If not, what could you do next time to make the lower magnet flip? Or if it did flip, what could you do to make it stay the same way up? Try out your ideas and see if you are right.

## Keep Thinking

Magnets are sometimes found in catches such as on cupboard doors and handbags. What do you think they are for and why do you think they are useful?

## Don't Stop There

● Take four identical ceramic ferrite magnets and stick them together to make two pairs. Use one pair to pull the other toward it, then to push the other away, as you did in steps 1 and 2. Does the magnetic force between the pairs feel stronger than it did between just two magnets?

# Is It a Magnet?

MAGNETS COME IN all shapes, colors, and sizes. It is not always easy to spot the real thing! In the next experiment you can find out whether your friends can tell which magnets are real and which are not.

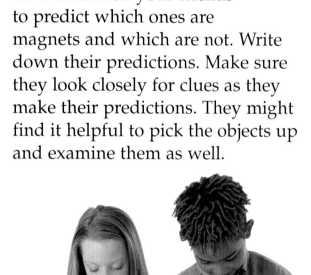

✓ **You will need**

✓ a selection of different magnets

✓ a selection of objects which are not magnets but look similar (such as a washer; ball of tin foil; silver cardboard; ball bearing)

✓ steel paper clips

**1** Put your selection of magnets and non-magnets on a table. Ask your friends to predict which ones are magnets and which are not. Write down their predictions. Make sure they look closely for clues as they make their predictions. They might find it helpful to pick the objects up and examine them as well.

**2** Now ask a friend to use paper clips to find out which objects are really magnets. Which objects picked up some clips and which did not? Make sure the experiment is fair by testing each object in the same way.

**3** Record the results by putting the magnets into one group and non-magnets into another.

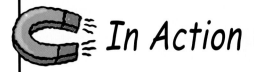 In Action

Magnetic strip is used in refrigerators to keep the door firmly shut. It is also used to display notices on magnetic display charts. Can you think of anything else that uses magnetic strip, and for what purpose it is used?

**4** Look back at your record of your friends' predictions. Were they all right or did you manage to trick them? Which clues helped them?

 Don't Stop There

● Look closely at some magnetic strip. What does it feel like? Is it very hard, quite hard, or soft? Is it rigid or flexible? Do you think it is a type of magnet? Test to find out using paper clips. Not all magnets are hard and rigid!

# How Strong Is a Magnet?

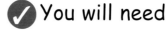

**M**AGNETS THAT PICK UP scrap cars are very strong, but magnets that hold a cupboard door closed are quite weak. Do this next experiment to find out about the strength of different magnets.

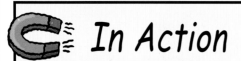

## In Action

Scientists use a machine called a magnetometer to measure magnetic strength in various materials. There are several types of magnetometers that can be used, depending on the material being measured in the experiment. Magnetometers give fast and accurate measurements.

**1** Which of the five magnets do you think is the strongest and which is the weakest? Look closely at the magnets and predict which one will hold the most paper clips and which will hold the least.

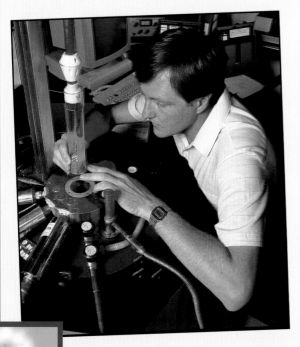

# Keep Thinking

Did you know that doctors use special magnets to pull out small steel splinters that get into people's eyes? Why do you think these magnets are used to pull out steel but not splinters of wood?

**2** Put the paper clips onto a table. Test each magnet to find out how many clips each will pick up. Keep a record of your results. Which was the strongest? Which was weakest? Was the biggest magnet the strongest?

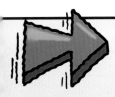

# Don't Stop There

● Take two identical ceramic ferrite magnets. Test to find out how many paper clips one magnet will pick up. Predict how many two magnets will pick up. Do you think two magnets will pick up twice as many? Test to find out.

● Have some fun designing and making magnetic models using magnets and colored magnetic objects. What can you make?

# Pick It Up!

**M**AGNETS WILL ONLY attract and pick up objects made of materials that contain iron, steel, nickel, or cobalt. These metals are magnetic. An object that is magnetic will be pulled by the magnetic force toward the magnet, then "stick" to it. Do this experiment to find out which materials are magnetic and which are not.

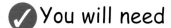

**1** Look closely at the materials and sort the objects into two groups, putting the ones you predict are magnetic in one pile and those you predict are not in another. Label each group clearly — one, "I predict these are magnetic" and the other, "I predict these are not magnetic."

**2** Now use the magnet to test your materials. Put the object being tested on a table. Hold the magnet high above the object and gradually lower it toward the object. Look closely to see if the magnet attracts the object and picks it up. Test each object in exactly the same way.

 **In Action**

Large magnets are used to help sort waste materials. The magnet (a type of electromagnet) is suspended on chains and is moved around by a crane. It is used to separate and lift heavy magnetic objects from among the waste.

**Keep Thinking**

Sometimes objects that are magnetic do not look like they are, because the iron or steel inside them is coated with a non-magnetic material such as plastic. Can you think of any examples of objects like this?

**3** Record your results by putting the materials into groups again. Re-label the groups clearly — "These are magnetic" and "These are not magnetic."

**4** Look closely at all the materials in each group. What did you find out? Which materials were magnetic? What did you find out? Were all of your predictions correct or did some results surprise you?

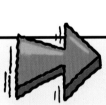

## Don't Stop There

● Make a fishing game. Cut fish shapes from cardboard and attach a different type of fastener (paper clips, adhesive tape, staple, paper fastener, safety pin) to each fish. Make fishing lines with pencils attached to string with a magnet on the end. Take turns to try and pull out a fish. Find out which fasteners are made of magnetic material and which are not.

# Stick Around!

**M**ANY OF THE OBJECTS around you are made of magnetic materials. To find out more about this try seeing what your magnet sticks to!

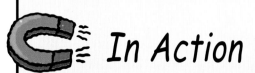 In Action

Some travel games such as chess have magnetic boards and magnets on the game pieces. This is to stop the pieces from wobbling around on a bumpy journey!

✔ You will need

✔ a magnet!

**SAFETY.** Before you do the experiment, check to make sure you are not near any televisions, computers, computer discs, tape recorders, CDs, video players, videotapes, or other sensitive equipment. You must not put your magnet on or near any of these objects as it can damage them!

**1** Look around your home or school and make a list of 10 surfaces or objects that you want to test to find out if a magnet will stick to them.

**2** Record your predictions in a table like the one below.

| LIST OF OBJECTS | MAGNETIC | NOT MAGNETIC |
|---|---|---|
|  |  |  |
|  |  |  |
|  |  |  |
|  |  |  |
|  |  |  |
|  |  |  |
|  |  |  |
|  |  |  |
|  |  |  |

## Keep Thinking

Adhesive tape will stick to a magnet but is not attracted to it. So is the tape a magnetic material?

**3** Now use your magnet to test the surfaces and objects and record your results in another table. Which surfaces and objects did the magnet stick to?

**4** Look at your results and think why the magnet stuck to some things and not others. Did the experiment you did on pages 12 and 13 help you to make accurate predictions? What materials do you think the magnetic surfaces and objects are made of?

## Don't Stop There

● What happens if you put a magnet nearer and nearer to a piece of modeling material? Does the magnet attract it? Can you use the magnet to pick it up? Do you think modeling material is magnetic? Wrap some modeling material around a magnet or a magnetic material. Do you think another magnet will pick it up? Try it and see.

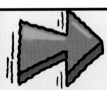

# The Invisible Force!

YOU CANNOT SEE THE magnetic force, but you know it is there because you can see and sometimes feel what it can do. Find out if this invisible force works through different materials.

**1** Set out the items to be tested in front of you. You will find it useful to have a record sheet to keep track of your results.

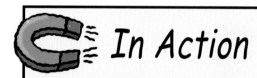

## ✓ You will need

- ✓ a strong bar magnet
- ✓ a selection of different materials which are not magnetic (eg: paper, thin cardboard, thick cardboard, thin wood, a book, fabric, glass, a plastic bag. Think of some others, too)
- ✓ steel paper clips or washers

**2** Take your magnet and a paper clip (or a washer), then place one of the non-magnetic items between them. Move the magnet around and see if the paper clip (or washer) moves in the same direction. Try it a few times until you are sure!

### ⊂Ξ In Action

Some windows are difficult to reach from the outside, so there is a tool for cleaning them which uses a magnet. It works through the glass, holding the two parts together as they are moved around to clean the inside and the outside of the window at the same time.

**3** Now try all the other materials in the same way. Do you think the thickness of the materials makes a difference? Were you surprised by any of your results?

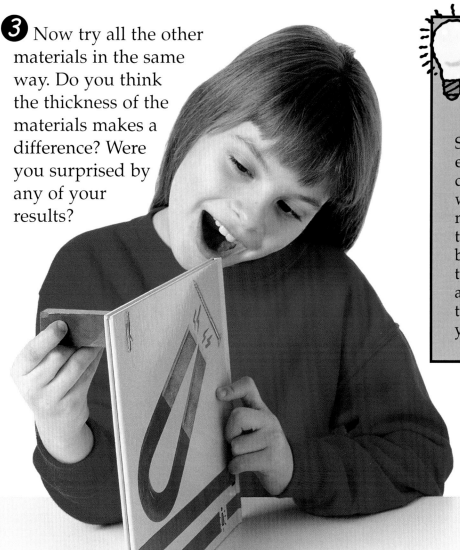

## Keep Thinking

Some machines or equipment can be damaged by magnetism working through the materials from which they are made. Look back at pages 14 and 15 to find out which things are sensitive and need to be kept away from your magnet.

**4** Do you think the magnet will work through your hand? Try it and find out! Also try and see if a magnet will work through your clothes.

## Don't Stop There

● A friend has dropped a paper clip into her glass of orange juice. Can you use your magnet to get it out without putting your hands in the juice?

● Make a game. Help the honeybee find the flower and return to the hive! On a piece of cardboard draw a route through a garden from a hive to a large flower. Cut out a picture of a bee and attach a steel paper clip to it. Use a magnet under the cardboard, to help the bee "fly" from the hive to the flower.

# From Pole to Pole

ARE BOTH ENDS OF A bar magnet the same? They may look the same, but try this experiment and you may be surprised when you find out more.

**You will need**
- ✓ two bar magnets
- ✓ a ruler

**1** Look closely at the bar magnets. Usually each half is a different color. The different ends are called the North pole and the South pole.

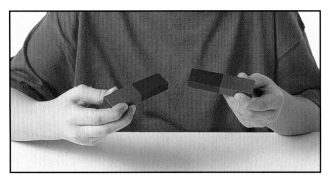

**2** Try to hold two ends of the same color (same poles) together. What do you notice? Do they attract and pull together or repel and push apart?

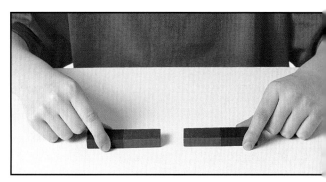

**3** Turn one magnet around and hold it against the other magnet again. Look closely to see what happens now.

**4** Turn the other magnet around so the opposite colors from step 2 face each other. What does this tell you about the poles of a magnet?

# In Action

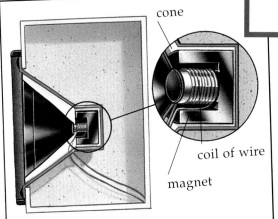

cone

coil of wire

magnet

● Magnets are used in many machines such as fans, hair dryers, and speakers. When electricity passes through a coil of wire in the machine, the coil becomes an electromagnet and vibrates between two other strong magnets. The poles of the magnets attract and repel the coil so that it moves around and makes the machine work. In a speaker, the magnets change some of the electric current in the wire into sound vibrations.

**5** Place one magnet next to a ruler in line with the zero. Put the other magnet, with the opposite pole facing the first one, at the far end of the ruler. Gently push this magnet toward the first one until they attract each other. Measure what the distance is when the magnets begin to move. Try it a few times.

**6** Now find out what the distance is when you make one magnet push the other one away.

 # Don't Stop There

● Where are the North and South poles on a horseshoe magnet? Using a bar magnet that has the North and South poles marked on it, slowly bring one end of the horseshoe magnet near to the North pole of the bar magnet. If the two magnets are attracted to each other, the pole of the horseshoe magnet is South. If the two magnets repel each other, then they have the same pole — North.

# Make Your Own Magnet!

D**ID YOU KNOW YOU CAN** make your own magnet? You need to use a strong magnet to make a new one. Magnets can be temporary (they don't remain magnetic) or they can be permanent. A material that can become either a temporary or a permanent magnet is made up of lots of tiny "mini-magnets" (called domains) all jumbled up inside it. When the material is made into a magnet, all the mini-magnets line up with all their poles facing the same direction.

✓ **You will need**
- ✓ a strong magnet
- ✓ a long steel nail
- ✓ some steel pins for testing (be careful with the pins)

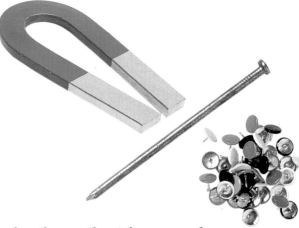

**1** First test the nail to be sure it is not a magnet by seeing if it will pick up the pins.

**2** Now stroke the nail with one pole of the magnet, in the same direction ONLY, between 30 and 40 times.

You must only use one pole of the magnet, so that the "mini-magnets" in the nail line up in the same direction.

20

## Keep Thinking

What else can you make magnetic? Is the new magnet temporary or permanent? Why does a magnet lose its magnetism? Think about those mini-magnets.

Magnets can be damaged in lots of ways, such as dropping, hitting, or heating them. Some magnets have a piece of magnetic metal called a keeper across the poles. Have you ever seen one? What do you think it is for?

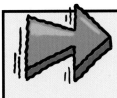

## Don't Stop There

● Drop your nail a few times on a hard floor or the ground. Ask an adult to supervise you. Now use the pins to test if it is still as strong. Keep dropping it and testing for strength. Is your magnet losing its strength?

**3** Test to see if the nail will pick up the pins. Look closely to see how many it will pick up. Have you made a magnet? Is it strong? How do you think you could make it stronger?

**4** Try stroking the nail again (in the same direction) another 20 times and see if it can pick up more pins. Have you made it stronger?

# Find the Force!

YOU HAVE TRIED LOTS of experiments with magnets in this book, but did you notice where on a magnet the magnetic force is strongest? Look back at pages 6, 7, 8, and 9 and think about what you found out then. Try some more experiments to find out where the strongest force is!

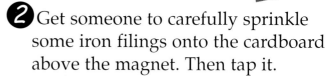

**1** First place the thin sheet of cardboard over the top of the bar magnet.

**2** Get someone to carefully sprinkle some iron filings onto the cardboard above the magnet. Then tap it.

**3** Look closely to see what happens. Can you see a pattern forming?

**4** Now move the magnet slightly and look closely as the iron filing pattern changes. The filings show the magnetic field of your magnet. Look closely to see where the filings bunch together — this shows you where there is a strong magnetic force field. Do you think the magnetic force is strongest at the poles or farther along the magnet?

**5** Repeat the experiment using different magnets. Are the patterns different? You can keep the magnetic field pattern as a picture if you carefully cover it with sticky backed plastic (ask an adult to help you).

## In Action

There are special machines used in hospitals that make use of a strong magnetic field. The patient lies in a magnetic field and a "picture" of their body can be seen on a screen. This body picture is called an MRI (magnetic resonance imaging) scan.

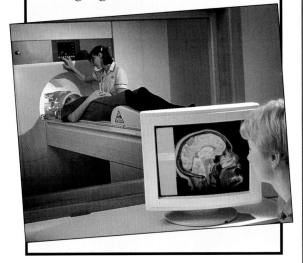

 ## Don't Stop There

● In the experiment on this page, you created a picture of a magnetic force field. Now try making a force field in a glass! Ask an adult to help you tie some thread around the center of a magnet and gently lower it into a transparent glass that has in it a mixture of iron filings stirred into glycerine (you can get this at the drug store), molasses, or baby oil. Look closely as the iron filings are gradually attracted to the magnet. Can you see where the force is strongest?

# Earth Is a Magnet, Too!

**Y**OU HAVE PROBABLY HEARD of the North and South poles of the Earth. Did you know they are a bit like the poles of a giant magnet, and that Earth has its own magnetic field? It is because of this magnetism that a compass needle points North or South. Make your own compass and try it out.

**1** Look back at pages 20 and 21 to see how to make a magnet. Make your needle into a magnet.

**2** Fix the needle to the cork or thin plastic with tape or Playdoh.

Look back at pages 20 and 21

## You will need

- ✓ a needle
- ✓ a thin slice of cork or piece of plastic sheet
- ✓ tape or Playdoh
- ✓ a magnet
- ✓ bowl of water
- ✓ a marker pen
- ✓ a compass for checking your homemade one!

**3** Carefully place your compass onto the surface of the water. Let it settle and stop moving. One end of the needle will point to the North and the other will point South. Use the bought compass to check which is the North end and then mark it 'N' with your marker pen.

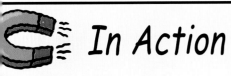 **In Action**

The Northern lights and Southern lights are magnificent natural effects seen in the night sky. They are partly caused by the Earth's magnetic field.

**4** Gently turn your homemade compass so it points in another direction, and then let it go. Look closely. Does it return to pointing North when it stops moving?

**Earth's Magnetic Field**
At the center of the Earth there is a core of liquid and solid iron. This is thought to cause Earth to act like a giant magnet, with its own magnetic poles. These poles are situated near the geographical North and South poles.
Earth's magnetic field is called the magnetosphere.

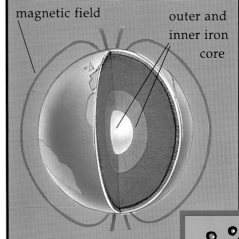

magnetic field

outer and inner iron core

**5** Now mark the other compass points (West, East, and South) on your homemade compass.

# Magnets from Electricity

IN **1820, A DANISH SCIENTIST** named Hans Christian Oersted discovered that a magnetic field was created when an electric current passed through a wire. This was a very important discovery because it led to the invention of the electromagnet. You can make one of these special types of magnets and see what it can do in this simple experiment.

## ✓ You will need
- ✓ single-strand insulated wire
- ✓ a pencil
- ✓ 4.5 volt battery
- ✓ wire stripper/scissors
- ✓ iron nail
- ✓ steel pins
- ✓ electrical tape

**SAFETY Use a battery for this experiment. NEVER use electricity.**

**1** Ask an adult to help you strip the insulating plastic from each end of the wire.

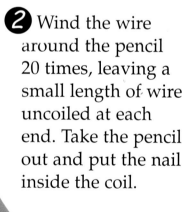

**2** Wind the wire around the pencil 20 times, leaving a small length of wire uncoiled at each end. Take the pencil out and put the nail inside the coil.

## *In Action*

Electromagnets are used in many machines, such as tape recorders, loudspeakers, electric doorbells, burglar alarms, telephones, some watches, and toasters (see page 19).
Maglev (magnetic levitation) trains (right) work using electromagnets. These magnets "lift" the train above the track so it can move along very quickly, quietly, and without causing pollution.

**3** Using the tape, attach the ends of the wire to the battery, one end to each terminal. An electric current is now passing through the wire

**4** With the current still flowing and the nail inside the coil, test to see if the nail is now a magnet. Will it pick up any pins? How many? Have you managed to make an electromagnet?

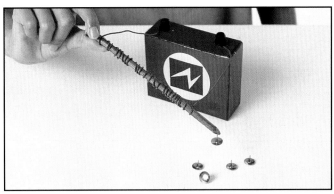

 ## *Don't Stop There*

● Repeat the experiment above. Now break the circuit so the current no longer flows, by detaching one end of the wire from the battery. What happens to the pins? Is the nail still a magnet?

● Make a bigger coil by winding a longer length of wire around a pencil 40 or 50 times. You may need some tape to hold the coil on the nail. Repeat the experiment above. How many pins will the electromagnet pick up now? Is it any stronger?

# Electricity from Magnets

A SCIENTIST NAMED Michael Faraday first discovered that magnets could be used to make electricity. You can do your own experiment to see this discovery in action. A dynamo for the lights on a bicycle works by using magnets. The magnet inside the dynamo turns inside a coil of wire when the wheels on the bicycle turn. This makes the electricity.

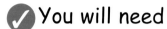

**✓ You will need**
- ✓ a bicycle
- ✓ a bicycle lamp with a dynamo

**1** Fix the dynamo lamp on to the bicycle. Ask an adult to help you.

**2** Get help to turn the bicycle upside down so that you can turn the pedal by hand. Ask a friend to hold the bike steady.

**3** Turn the pedal slowly and watch the lamp. Does the light come on as soon as the pedal turns or after a little while? What happens if you turn the pedal faster?

**4** Find out by turning the pedal slowly, then faster, and then very fast. Look closely at the brightness of the light each time. Record your results in a table like this one (right).

| | BRIGHTNESS | | |
|---|---|---|---|
| **PEDALLING** | | NO LIGHT | DIM LIGHT | BRIGHT LIGHT |
| | SLOW | | | |
| | FAST | | | |
| | VERY FAST | | | |

## Don't Stop There

● Now see if you can measure the speed the pedals must turn to make the light very bright. You will need to put a little sticker on the edge of the wheel to act as a marker. Use the marker to count the number of turns needed in a certain time (say 5 seconds) to light up the lamp. Try doing this a few times.

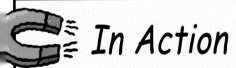

**5** What did you find out? Were you surprised? What happens to the light when the wheel stops turning?

## In Action

When electricity is produced in large amounts, such as to light your home or school, or in power stations, magnets are used in huge generators. Without the magnets they would not work.

# Glossary

The meaning of each word, as it is used in this book.

**Attract** If a magnet attracts a material or another magnet it can pull it toward it and pick it up.

**Bar magnet** A magnet in the shape of a bar.

**Ceramic ferrite magnet** A strong dark gray magnet which comes in a variety of different shapes.

**Cobalt** A hard, strong magnetic metal.

**Compass** A device with a magnetized swinging needle that always points North.

**Dynamo** A machine that uses magnetism to make electricity.

**Electric current** A flow of electricity through an electrical circuit.

**Electric motor** A machine used to turn things, worked by electricity.

**Electricity** A type of energy used to heat things, light things, and make things work.

**Electromagnet** A special type of magnet made using electricity.

**Experiment** A fair test done to find out more about something or answer a question. Sometimes

called an investigation.

**Flexible** A material that is flexible is easy to bend, and it doesn't break.

**Force** A force is something that pushes or pulls an object and makes it move. The force can change the direction or the shape of the object.

**Generator** A machine that produces electrical energy.

**Horseshoe magnet** A magnet made in the shape of a horseshoe.

**Insulated wire** A metal wire with a plastic covering.

**Iron** A silvery colored metal that is used to make steel. It is a common magnetic material.

**Iron filings** Little pieces of iron.

**Keeper** A thin bar of iron placed across the poles of some magnets to keep the magnet strong.

**Lodestone (or magnetite)** A type of rock that is also a magnet. Magnetism gets its name from this rock.

**Maglev (magnetic levitation) train** A train that moves along very quickly using electromagnets.

**Magnetic** If a magnet attracts a material then the material is magnetic.

**Magnetic field** The area around a magnet where its force can be felt or detected.

**Magnetic poles** A magnet has two poles, North and South. The magnetic force is strongest at the poles.

**Magnetic strip** A thin strip of material that is a magnet, so it sticks to a magnetic surface.

**Magnetism** An invisible force that attracts magnetic materials.

**Magnetosphere** The magnetic field surrounding the Earth, reaching far out into space.

**Material** The substance or the "stuff" that things are made of like air, water, wood, rock, glass, metal, or fabric.

**MRI (magnetic resonance imaging) scan** A technique used by doctors that uses a magnetic field to make special pictures of the insides of people's bodies.

**Nickel** A hard, strong magnetic metal.

**Permanent** If something changes permanently it will always stay changed and will never go back to what it was like before.

**Predict** To guess what will happen in an experiment before doing it.

**Repel** If one pole of a magnet repels another it will push it away and the poles will not stick together.

**Result** The outcome of an experiment.

**Rigid** A material that is rigid will not bend.

**Steel** A hard silvery-gray mixture of materials including iron.

**Temporary** Something which happens only for a short time.

**Transparent** If a material is transparent it means that it is completely see-through.

# Index